HOW BADLY DO YOU WANT IT?

A Married Couple's Guide to a
Healthy & Passionate Marriage.

Wilber & Quashaunda Kitchens

Published by Quashaunda Kitchens

Printed in the United States of America

Cover photography 2022 by David Mahone.

Library of Congress Control Number: 2023902476

ISBNs:
979-8-9877510-0-8 (print)
979-8-9877510-1-5 (eBook)

A strong marriage requires two people who choose to love each other even on the days they struggle to like each other.

Visit www.thekitchenstable.com/sidenotes
For more resources to help you effectively
communicate with your spouse.

The one thing that has sustained us is we agreed early in the marriage that we wouldn't discuss our issues with family or friends, nor would we ever call the law to our home. My wife once mentioned to me that she didn't get married to get a divorce, that stuck with me. February 18, 2023 will be 33 years married and 35 years total. Marriage is hard work loving someone more than yourself is satisfying.

~ G. Anderson

Give grace and space to learn and grow in the journey of marriage.

~ S. Carter (female)

Dedication

To our children,
Makiel Kitchens
Kentrell Kitchens
Kaydence Kitchens
Kiya Chandler
Nakyra Hill

From the book
The Role of I in Commitment

"Our spouses see the true depths of our character. Regardless of how much we say we love God, they see our love for God in how we interact with them, speak with them, and love them. Then their behaviors become a reflection of that character. Plainly stated, we are a reflection of our spouse's behavior and likewise they are a reflection of ours."

~ D. Harris (female)

Often reminisce on what got you all together and revisit some of the places and share the memories with kids and family. Make each other laugh. Share desired activities. (We work out every morning at 4:30am). Know that one mate can't win all of the battles. Try to be friends first if possible. Keep others out of your business whether it's good or bad.

~ D. Lewis (male)

Contents

A Prayer for your spouse,
This is one of the beautiful and encouraging prayers Wilber sent to his wife Quashaunda when he was working out of state. Take time to think of a beautiful and encouraging prayer to pray over your spouse.

Good morning, Beautiful! Watched the Lakers series last night and fell asleep watching, it was not on purpose! You know I yearn for our telephone time. I need it! Praying this morning for God to continue to use me to continue to keep me leaning on His word. I pray that no distractions steer me away from his leadership. While being led by God I'm able to lead my family in the right direction by staying consistent and disciplined. Allow me to continue leading my family by setting an example. Cover my family Lord, protect them, give them strength to go on with their day-to-day task and keep them safe from any harm. Father, I can't thank you enough for my beautiful wife, continue to bless her. Bless her hands to be the best esthetician that she can be. Thank you, Lord, for her resilience and her drive. Give her the strength to keep her going so all of our brands and endeavors are successful in Your name. Bless and heal our grandson. Heal his body of any ailments bless Kaydence to be the star that she is. Allow her to be a sponge and learn all she can. In Jesus' name we pray.

Amen!

Introduction

Welcome to *How Badly Do You Want It? A Married Couple's Guide to A Healthy & Passionate Marriage* and thank you for purchasing this book. Our hope is that by the time you finish reading this book, you will have the strategies and knowledge to work on and improve your marriage intentionally.

If you are reading this book, then we know that you're ready to have the healthy and passionate marriage that you desire. However, you can't seem to make it happen with what you've already been doing. You've been struggling with finding the strength and confidence to put in the work needed to improve your marriage. Having a blended family can be very difficult to navigate. We've experienced this first hand with having two kids outside our marriage and at the time, we had two kids of our own. The scheduling of birthday parties, holiday time, and school functions can be overwhelming. Getting those phone calls in the wee hours of the morning because your sick child needs to go to the ER has happened in our marriage. We also have had to deal with the emotional and financial support the child needs. This can be downright exhausting. It's always something!

Let's face it. None of us is a mind reader. However, you expect your spouse to read your mind, and that's just not fair. Therefore, learn how to communicate your needs and desires effectively to your spouse to avoid unnecessary fights when the "need" you have not communicated effectively is not met.

Overwhelming financial burdens placed on one spouse can be a sure way to a divorce. Not having and sticking to a budget is a recipe for disaster. Discover which spouse is more financially responsible and let that person be in control of the finances, so you don't end up homeless. However, both parties still must work together and contribute financially for the well-being of your household, so the financial strain is not all on one person. Before we understood this and put it into practice, we experienced every financial disaster you could think of. Once we finally did this, the pressure was released, and the peace flowed.

We wrote this book to show you that it is possible to have the marriage you desire. We give you the tools and knowledge, so you, too, can overcome your challenges and improve your marriage. Don't give up! We're here to guide you along the way. Even before writing our book, we have advised and provided guidance to other married couples in similar situations.

The Kitchens Table 2.0. What does that mean, you ask? Well, this is our second marriage to each other. The first marriage was August 21, 1999 at the young and naïve age of twenty-one and twenty-two. It lasted just shy of ten years. Our second and current marriage began on February 15, 2019, and it has been a 180-degree turnaround. Now, it's not perfect. However, it is a slice of heaven compared to some of the hell we experienced.

Our marriage is so much better. Our communication comes with ease now. Our finances have improved a great deal, and together, we purchased our dream home, but it wasn't always this way. We remember when arguing and blow ups were all too familiar. Unspoken expectations and comparisons were like a raging fire in our marriage. With all this going on, tension, affection, and intimacy often took a back seat.

For myself, Wilber, counseling sessions were a great start to get the ball rolling. However, I had to take my own advice. I began to put in the work and stay consistent. Leading by example and trusting the process is how I implemented my own teachings. After going through our divorce, which felt like "walking death," a win for me now is waking up every day to my wife, the love of my life. A renewed mindset is where the breakthrough started. Then, we made the necessary adjustments, and ten years later, we're remarried. I began to get my life in order. I focused on being a better man, so I could be a better husband and father for my family. Being led by God first allowed me to lead my family, so we could be successful in all areas of our lives.

Because I was able to make the mindset shift, I, Quashaunda, began to show up as the wife I knew I could be, the wife my husband desired and the wife I wanted to be. As his wife, I had to make the mindset shift to not let past hurts hold me back from fully loving my husband. This allowed me to live in the moment and have hope for our future. I enjoy the improved relationships with my husband and our children due to our ability to communicate effectively. With the help of God, we followed the process, and we are still able to stand together, holding hands, smiling, and loving one another.

The purpose of *How Badly Do You Want It? A Married Couple's Guide to A Healthy & Passionate Marriage* is to help keep marriages together and strong. We want to share our experiences and give you the tools and prayers to build or repair your marriage. We've taken the same strategies that we used to heal and rebuild our own marriage and placed them in this book for you. We're living proof that with God, you can turn your marriage around. Like us, you must do the work to get your desired result. Yes, it may seem like a task at first but rejoice in knowing that God makes all things new. He can bring new life to a dying marriage. Do not relive and call to mind hurt from the past. Doubt and procrastination only will lead to more stress and arguments and less communication and intimacy. Instead, renew your mind to look ahead and be excited about the new and good things to come in your marriage.

What God put together, let no man destroy! You've purchased this book because you know that your marriage is not over. You know that you and your spouse still love each other deeply. Once you read *How Badly Do You Want It? A Married Couple's Guide to A Healthy & Passionate Marriage,* you will be refreshed and equipped with a new outlook on your marriage. We're here for you, and we want to help you get to the healthy and passionate marriage you desire. It will require some work and mindset shifts, but you can do it!

The Kitchens Table
Love Happens Here.
Wilber & Quashaunda

CHAPTER 1

Seek God First

" Though one may be overpowered, two can defend themselves. A cord of three strands is not quickly broken." Ecclesiastes 4:12. The cord of three strands represents the husband and the wife. The braiding of these symbolizes the joining of man, woman, God, and marriage. It was August 21, 1999 at Salem Baptist Church when a young twenty-one-year-old and twenty-two-year-old in love and naïve couple stood before God and a packed church and said, "I do." This was the official beginning of our journey into marriage, a world in which we quickly learned why God needs to be in the center of it.

Wilber speaking: I met her once upon a time, but I chose her three times. I chose her the moment I saw her, not to sound cliché. It was my freshman year at Southwest Dekalb High School. I was in the trombone section of one of the best bands in the South. What can I say? I remember the day like it was yesterday when I saw this fine young lady walk in the band room with that black dress. Oh, I can still see her outfit with black tights, and they fit so nicely. I had to know her name. I had to know who she was. This particular afternoon while sitting in the trombone section in the band room, she walked in wearing a black dress. I came down from my trombone section and quickly and confidently approached her to introduce myself. She was shy and reserved but classy and well-put-together. I've learned from watching other women in my life that a woman's clothes tell a lot about who she is. To that extent, she was neat, meticulous, and detail-oriented. Her skin was well taken care of, not troubled with acne. She had smooth even ridges of chocolate mocha made from cocoa butter, simply beautiful.

Her response to my introduction was pleasant and receptive. In the days that followed, I grew more and more fond of her with every meeting. After a couple of months, we started to go together. We went to her house where she introduced me to her family; I learned that we had even more in common. Our family values seem to align perfectly. It was also good to see how well her mother had preserved her youthfulness. I got to see a peek into what I could anticipate for the future. However, this did not last as long as I had hoped. I was so happy to be in a relationship with her, but high school proved challenging. We made a lot of mistakes. Hearts were bruised. Feelings were hurt. Trust was broken.

Sophomore year, we headed down separate paths. With no social media in the nineties, we relied heavily on simple cameras to record all our best moments that pictured our dope outfits and our best friendships. There was a photo studio called Harris, famous for its white columns and soft finish that everyone frequented to take pictures. You haven't lived until you've returned to school with new pictures and handed out as many autographs as you could with a meaningful message on the back of the photo.

I remember one autograph on the back of a picture that I gave to Shaunda. It said, "You will be my wife." Thinking back to the signature on that picture, I am moved to tears today. Those words weren't just words. They were my prayers. But God. Years later as a freshman in college, I had lost all contact with her. I had not forgotten that five-word prayer scribbled on the back of that Harry's wallet-sized picture. I was downtown one day, and I bumped into one of her sisters. I immediately asked, "Hey, where's your sister?" I handed her my number, which I'm sure must have been a beeper number, and I insisted that she pass it along. I now know that it was God. He is the light, the truth, and the connector. I'd been given the opportunity to choose her again a second time, and I did.

We reunited and things went well. Even with the ups and downs, it was during this time I discovered my wife. I chose her because she was everything that I was not. One day, I came over to her house, and I remember vividly what she was doing. I walked in and she was writing on something that looked like a little book. I asked her, "What are you doing?" She was balancing her checkbook. I thought to myself, *Oh my gosh, she's getting the money right down to the penny.* I knew a little about money. I mainly knew how to get it fast and spend it just as quickly. It was not my strong point. This was a moment I knew I needed her. I chose her a third time at that moment. Balancing a checkbook at nineteen was next level. I can recall going to work and returning with all my money. I insisted that she manage my finances as well. She was my better half. She was the one.

It wasn't until after the divorce that I realized what it meant to seek God first. The emotion was real. A lot of people asked me, "How did it feel? Why did y'all get a divorce? What happened?" It felt like a walking death. I was unable to have my family or my kids. I was a hands-on dad, so I enjoyed being able to be there every day. The things that I missed so much were taking my kids to school, doing homework, and going to football practices. I even missed going up to the school for a parent-teacher conference. That was very important to me; it allowed me to be a husband and father.

When the divorce happened, I was pretty much a single man. I conducted myself like a single person would. I partied a lot. I hung out a lot. However, I always kept faith in God that He would see me through those hard times. I can remember times when I wouldn't be able to talk to my wife. I couldn't see her because, at those times, I would question, *What is she doing where she's at? She's out in the world doing whatever she wants to do, how she wants to do it, and with whomever she wants to do it.* I had no control over it. I had to come to grips with that. However, for me to focus on what I needed to do, I had to become a better person. I just had to. I would tell people I wanted her to want me. I wanted her to feel proud that she chose me as her husband. I didn't want to make her want me by being pushy.

I wanted to be the one she sought out and desired. I had to position myself in that light to be the one for her or for anybody in that state because it wasn't her that I was pursuing. We were divorced. I just wanted to be better as a person. I had to reinvent myself. I had to get more focused. I got more focused with my career and my goals. Our financial situation had to get better, not just for her but for me as a man. You must take care of yourself first before you can take care of someone else. My faith was there. That was the only way I got through that time in my life. Going through a divorce is like a walking death.

Once I got past the hurt, I was more at ease with actually going through the divorce. It was not as hard as I thought because I still believed that God would see me through it, and it was going to be okay. I was at a comfortable place in my heart and mind. The day we got divorced, it was a strange day to say the least. We rode together to the courthouse. While we were waiting for our name to be called up for our case, a big storm came through the DeKalb County Courthouse, and the power went out in the entire courthouse. They informed us that we'd have to go into the hallway and wait for the storm to pass. I was believing in God. I said to myself that it clearly was a sign that we should just leave. I asked her if she wanted to leave because to me, it was a sign that we shouldn't be doing it. I was standing on my faith and believing in God. When you believe in God, you give Him full authority to deliver what it is you've requested. You are not worried about the how, when, what, or where of a situation. You just know that in due time, He will give you the desires of your heart. I believed God was saying, "Hey, I don't want y'all to get a divorce." How could a storm of this magnitude come at the time when we were going to finalize our divorce; it was ironic.

The lights eventually came back on, and we went in. We were cordial when we spoke in front of the judge. He asked her some direct questions about how I was as a man. He asked her if she thought that I would still be a part of our kids' lives. She told him that I would. He was lenient on the final disposition of the arrangements as far as how much child support and alimony I'd have to pay. That part went well. We finalized the divorce. I still had to take some parenting classes because Shaunda is strictly by the book, and she already had taken her courses. I had been dragging my feet, but that didn't stop her determination to go through with it. The judge told her that if anything happened, and I did not do my part, she could come and see him person-ally, and he would make sure that I suffered the consequences by law. He was stern, but that's the court system. They're going to go with the woman's side. Needless to say, it turned out to be a pleasant divorce. We left the courthouse together, and I went back to her apartment because I was sleeping in my car, and I didn't have any place to call home. We were together one last time. Again, that was God saying to me, "Relax, I got you. Just work on yourself and put Me first."

Quashaunda speaking: Initially, I chose Wilber based on his looks and charm. He was fine. Yes, I was wearing that black dress that day in the band room, and I do mean wearing it. Yeah, I was sure he noticed me. I noticed him previously as well. He'd been hanging around in the band room before class on occasion, and of course, I'd see him during practices, but we never had a conversation. That day, he introduced himself. I came face to face with the charm I'd only noticed from a distance. Wilber stayed fresh, Polo fresh from head to toe to compliment his looks and charm. His skin was smooth and dark. He was clean cut with an athletic build. He stood, chest up and shoulders back, and he was a true people person. He talked to everyone.

When we finally met in the band room, his conversation was short and sweet. I don't really remember what he said, but I remember the way he made me feel special. He left me blushing and waiting for our next conversation. It wasn't long before I was all in. We went in, full speed ahead. We were boyfriend and girlfriend, sharing lockers, skipping class to be in each other's lunch period. We shared candy grams and movie dates. What drew me closer to him was how he made me feel special. He was proud to be my boyfriend. He was a real gentleman, opening doors and complimenting me on my looks. He would make sure that I was straight. We always had a really good time. We were friends.

Wilber comes from a large, close-knit family, so there was always a family gathering, and everyone knew who I was and treated me accordingly. The love he felt for me carried into how his family treated me and respected me as his girlfriend. However, being teenagers in love, the roller coaster ride was fun, but it soon came to a stop. We were fourteen and fifteen, so that high school heartbreak was sure to come. Who knew that a little over a year later, we would pick back up where we left off. We were a little older in age and a little more mature. The relationship this time was the "sweep you off your feet" type. His physique had matured. The cologne, the cars, the swag, the gifts, the dates, and everything else was so much better; we were on and popping before this "Do it for the Gram" era. We were fly! Lol! My little sister used to steal his Polo and Nautica shirts and wear them to MBK (My Brother's Keeper) teen club. You have to be from Atlanta to know about MBK. We were always together on the scene from Decatur to Atlanta. Our love once again blossomed. It was so beautiful and so strong, yet we still had so much to learn.

Thank God, I grew up as a kid in church, the. Church of God in Christ (C.O.G.I.C.) to be specific, so I knew how to call on the name of Jesus when times got hard. That was evident in the first part of our marriage because although our wedding day was beautiful, our actual marriage would prove to be not as pretty. Celebrating our love with our family and friends, wearing my beautiful wedding gown from David's Bridal, and enjoying my special day with our bridesmaids, groomsmen, and my sexy husband, August 21, 1999, was a beautiful day. However, it was also a bitter day, because it was one year ago to the date one of his daughters was born. I only found this out later into the planning of our wedding. In fact, I initially chose August 28, but that date was unavailable. That day carried a bittersweet memory, and it was in the beginning of our marriage that I knew I had to seek God first and often.

Having a personal relationship with God is the key to having a successful marriage. Growing up in the church, I have a personal relationship with God, and I know the power of prayer. I've felt His presence working in my life on several occasions. Thanking Him daily and praising Him in the good and the bad times is how I live my life. It's how I've gotten through victories and tribulations. Your foundation with God will help you make decisions in your life that will honor and sustain your marriage instead of allowing it to be destroyed. Praying was something that we did often, and we needed it often. We went to church together, and we raised our kids in the church.

Be true to yourself about what you really want and why you want it. Ask God to align your walks with His will and let His will be done in your life. Staying in the will of God is what will bring and keep the peace in your life and marriage. Keeping this in the forefront will help to eliminate a lot of second guessing and create the healthy and passionate marriage that you desire. Your marriage always will present times when you need to go to God in prayer. He promised to never leave us or forsake us, so in good times, thank Him, and in difficult times, seek Him.

We have had equally good and bad times and I thank God that we knew how to pray when we needed to pray, and we knew how to thank Him in advance for what He had done and what He was doing in our marriage. We thanked Him and appreciated the times when we were able to see that our prayers had been answered and favor was on our marriage.

CHAPTER 2

Pray With and For Your Spouse

As persons of faith, praying to God for our needs and desires to be met is an integral part of our life. Prayer for your spouse and with your spouse helps you connect with your spouse on a deeper level because this is a place where you both can be vulnerable and make your requests known to God. Knowing that you are children of God and believing in what you request in prayer will give you even more faith and belief that what you ask, He will bring to pass.

Quashaunda speaking: At my previous work location, West Midtown Atlanta to be exact, I was fed up with what was going on from the distance to the tension in the workplace with coworkers. It was really a straight shot from my house, which was south of the airport, to where I worked. If you know Atlanta, you know you could take one street to get from one side of town to the other. However, with everyone now moving to Atlanta, the city was growing tremendously, and traffic was a nightmare getting to work. Our daughter, Kaydence, was in elementary school, so I was rushing back and forth to get her from school on time while still trying to grow my business and take clients in the evening. You can see where my frustration with traffic came from.

With my coworkers, the tension was more so caused by the fact that we were in each other's space. I have my own skincare business, Complexions Skincare & Beauty. However, while transitioning from a family-owned business to an independent business, there was a brief period where I had to operate my business inside another salon. Sometimes with women in the beauty industry, we just don't see eye to eye on certain things. Plus, it was just time for me to have my own space. The feeling was magnified. You can double, triple, or quadruple that. With that being said, my days of wanting to go to work were decreasing, even though I loved what I did. I was passionate about what I did. I sometimes hated going to work because I knew these were two major things that I was going to have to deal with, so I expressed these concerns with my husband, and he began to pray for me that this situation would change for the better. He was actually the one to find the location where my business is located now. On his way to work, he would pass by what is now my current location for my business.

We met with the owner of the building one Thursday. He told us to think about it over the weekend. As we thought about it, we also prayed about it. We prayed that our decision would bring peace in my business and peace within me, so there could be peace in our marriage. We all know that when there's no peace in the workplace, it's hard to have peace in the house. We believed that God would answer our prayers. On the following Monday, we made the decision to move forward with the new location. I did the work with city hall and made sure that everything was okay. I got permits in place and paid the required deposits. I resigned (not necessarily resigned), and I advised the owner of the salon where I was working that it would be my last week. I cleaned my space on Wednesday and packed up Thursday. I started servicing my clients at my new location on Friday. Prayer really does change things. Moreover, I've been able to grow my business in this location. I've been here since 2018. That's over four years, and my business has grown like it's never grown before. Pray without ceasing. Sometimes, the answer doesn't always come when we want it, but it will come when we need it.

When you are praying with and for your spouse, give thanks for them and encourage them and pray for God's blessing and protection over their life. When there has been turmoil in your marriage, pray that God will heal your marriage and restore the peace and love you have for one another. This is how you keep your marriage strong. This is how we've kept our marriage strong, even though the disagreements may come. I'm glad that we're at a place now that we understand the power of prayer and the importance of praying together. We are at a place now where we put our egos aside and really pray and find out what the problem is. We always come out on the other side, the better side.

Wilber speaking: When I work out of town, my schedule is very different from my wife's schedule. I'm up around 5:00 a.m. My wife is not a morning person; she's normally up around 8:00 a.m.. By that time, I am deep into my work with meetings and training, and I am just getting the crews ready to go to work. I can't stop to talk on the phone to pray with my wife, so I came up with a solution. I started to pray in the morning when I woke up, and I would send that actual prayer to my wife, so she could see the prayer as if I was standing there with her holding hands and saying the prayer. It feels good to know that when she gets up, she can see the prayer. She knows that no matter how far away I am from her, we say a prayer as if we were together. That allows me to go throughout my day knowing that I've covered my family and poured into them, and I've asked God to protect them when I'm not there. As a husband, my job is to protect our family. This allows me to know and feel confident that no matter what goes on today, my family is protected.

Working out of town was my way to provide for my family. At times, I felt lonely, and FaceTime calls just weren't enough. I turned to my faith and prayed to God for something better that could bring me closer to my family. Instead of saying that I was tired of working out of town, I kept working, staying positive, and praying to God for a job in which I could work from home. Three months later, I received a job offer for me to work remotely. I saw God's hand at work in my life again. It allowed me to be home to be there for my kids, take them to school, pick them up, attend practices, cook breakfast in the morning, and just be the dad that I needed to be.

When going to God in prayer for your marriage, you first must trust and believe that God will answer your prayer. Having this mindset will allow you to have peace and allow you to wait on God until your answer comes. In closing, we have a short, yet effective prayer for your spouse.

Heavenly Father, you brought my spouse and me together. That is why we come boldly before you and before your throne asking you to heal our marriage. Infuse us with a passion for life, love, intimacy, and passion to grow in wisdom and serve you together. Teach me how to build them up rather than tear them down. Allow me to create a space for their emotional, mental, and spiritual growth in a way that supports their health. Bless their coming and going and grant them favor and all their doings. Let them feel the love that I have for them on this day and forevermore. Amen.

CHAPTER 3

R-E-S-P-E-C-T

One of the most important factors in your marriage is respect. In fact, respect is downright crucial in a marriage. It often ranks right beside or sometimes higher than love when it comes to the success of a marriage. Is it really possible to love someone that you don't respect? Is it possible to be married to someone you don't respect? We feel it's equally as important as love. Respect is as healthy as love is passionate. Respect is both verbal and action-oriented. It means that you treat your spouse in a thoughtful and caring manner. You avoid disrespect at all costs. Refrain from being combative towards your spouse or undermining them during conflict. Couples should respect each other and share their own feelings, opinions, and interests without the fear of being judged or rejected by their spouse. Although it is of high importance, respect sometimes is lost in communication and action. Respect yourself and your spouse in all aspects of your marriage.

Family functions can go south really quickly because this principle is not followed. In-laws are notorious for treating a spouse less than they should, making the spouse feel disrespected because of what a family member has told them regarding their marriage. In some cases, the disrespect can be due to the relationship that an in-law has developed with the spouse's previous partner. Even when the two of you have made up, in-laws can still hold that grudge so keep your business to yourself. There may be times that an in-law is holding on to an ex-partner and keeps bringing that person around and inviting the person to family functions. There must be boundaries set regarding this situation to keep peace in your marriage.

Wilber speaking: I come from a large, close-knit family, and we always are having a function for something – baby showers, graduations, weddings, birthdays, or family reunions. Any type of party, you name it, there's always a reason to celebrate. My mom has been known to be one of the matriarchs or the matriarch of the family. She's the one who everybody goes to for whatever they need. She's the one who everybody loves. She has a big heart of gold. She always wants to give to people and make them feel good. She likes to have everybody around her, no matter what. Sometimes, I feel like she needs the attention. She craves it, and that can be a bad thing, especially for me as her son, who has children who are not by my wife. She has created relationships with the mothers of my other kids as well, and this caused tremendous problems in our first marriage. When my daughters were babies, it was common for the mothers to drop our daughters off or pick them up when it was my turn to spend time with them or vice versa. I would be the one to pick them up or drop them off. However, the problems occurred when my mom would have a function, sometimes not even her function, and because she's that person, she wants everybody to attend. She wants everybody around her.

My wife and I, young in our marriage with our two sons in tow, would be invited to those same family functions. We were ready to enjoy our day, spend time with our family, laugh, and have a good time. Well, to our surprise, when we got there, lo and behold, my mother took it upon herself to invite the mothers of my other children. This created a boatload of issues between my wife and me. What do we do? Do we leave the function that we're invited to attend? Do we sit there and try to brush it off? Do I act like my wife is not irritated? Or what? This left me infuriated with my mom! Yes, I love my mom. However, I love my wife as well, and I refused to allow her to be disrespected. I explained to my mother that this behavior would not be tolerated because it made my wife feel uneasy. It was something that I had to grow and mature to do because being young and still under the rule of my mother's thumb, I didn't know whom I was supposed to please.

Oftentimes, I was caught in the middle between a rock and what I thought was a hard place. I did not want to mess up the relationship with my children. Yet, I did not want to bring discord into my home either. I would just close up. I would have arguments with my wife, telling her that she was my wife, and she should be the bigger person because my mom just wanted to be around her grandchildren. However, I didn't realize that my mom was being manipulative in this manner by bringing the mothers of those children to the event when it was unnecessary. Having a blended family can be difficult. For us, it was something that we constantly were learning to navigate. I was just trying to keep the peace with the mothers of my daughters, so I could build a relationship with my daughters and acknowledge my wife's feelings and position. I fought hard with myself to not be like my biological father in the way of being absent. My vulnerability in this position made me feel like I was being manipulated on one hand. However, my wife being treated like the unwanted stepdaughter when she was a child made her feel vulnerable. She was subjected to a lot of unnecessary drama, and it started to eat away at the trust she had in me to keep her as my top priority.

Husbands, a good scripture to reference concerning respect for your wife is 1 Peter 3:7. Husbands, in the same way be considerate as you live with your wives, and treat them with respect as the weaker partner and as heirs with you of the gracious gift of life, so that nothing will hinder your prayers.

Quashaunda speaking: This second time around in our marriage has been easier for me to respect my husband's decisions. We already overcame so many more areas of disrespect. I had to deal with the disrespect that happened among myself, his mother, and the mothers of his children because it was not clear who comes first, who's respected first, and whose respect is held in highest regard. Previously, it felt like war because he had no example of this type of situation. His mother didn't have to deal with any other children or their mothers outside the marriage to his stepfather (the man who raised him since a little boy). Not knowing how to navigate through these types of situations properly felt like I constantly was having to fight for my respect as his wife. I had to fight with all of them. Because there still may have been feelings of love there or feelings of anger from the mothers of his other children, I felt the disrespect. From being negatively discussed on social media to having to see them at family functions and hear the whispers to being the last one to know when one of the children needed to come live with us, which happened on more than one occasion. When one of his children had to come live with us, I would be the main caregiver, but I was not given the respect to know until the child was already there. This level of disrespect made me feel less than a wife. I felt undervalued and used. I had to really pray and reassure myself that I was worthy. I had thoughts of ending it all and saying, "To hell with everyone, particularly my husband. Let's see how you handle this without me." Those feelings became a constant, vivid thing. I stayed in prayer because I knew I didn't want to go out like that, but I wanted it to STOP!

The ONLY thing that kept me sane was my children. Those precious baby boys who I loved with all my heart deserved a healthy, sane, and loving mother, and I refused to give that away. I was not about to give away my biggest blessing to anyone else by ending my life. I knew that they needed their mother, and they were my fuel to keep going. I refused to let anyone, even my husband, drive me to the point of suicide for something that they didn't even realize they were doing. He didn't understand the magnitude of the pain that his actions caused. This is why effective communication and mutual respect between a HUSBAND and WIFE is so important. I really had to let go and let God. I stopped worrying about things that I couldn't control. I let go of everyone's perceptions about me, except for my children and myself. I got baptized in our church shortly afterwards and rededicated my life to God. I began to regain a level of peace, value, and respect for myself.

Early in our first marriage, position and placement were unclear or sometimes unvalued. Saturdays were the one day of the week where we had an opportunity to enjoy most of our leisure plans. Will and I had our day set to spend time together with our boys. Then, we would end the evening with just the two of us. However, receiving a phone call early in the morning from his mother with her own agenda put him between what he thought was a rock and a hard place. Being immature in this type of situation, he wondered, *Whom do I please? My mom, whose house I just left. The woman who's taken care of me my entire life or my wife? The woman I vowed before God to love, who is the mother of my children and my partner for life.* His choice was, "Let me go help my mom and then come back home." Well, a couple of hours turned into all day, and you already can imagine that at home that night was not pretty. This type of consistent battling can tear away at marriages for sure. However, now in The Kitchens 2.0, priorities and boundaries are understood by all parties. This is no longer an issue. Emergencies are one thing, but home comes first, and this goes both ways.

Setting boundaries for your marriage is key to protecting both of you from being taken advantage of and losing trust. Healthy relationships with co-parenting is possible. In marriage, your spouse is your top priority. Your spouse's feelings should be valued, and their trust should not be jeopardized. As the non-biological parent in a blended family, you accept and love the kids as a parent; however, you do not have to tolerate disrespect. It is so much easier to lead with love. Over the years, watching my husband be an active father in his daughters' lives is what I knew they all needed. When I supported him with his parental responsibilities, I showed him that he could trust me to love and care for his daughters as my own. I led with love and genuine concern for the girls. I knew what it felt like to be treated like a stepchild, and I did not want them to experience that from. I also did not want them to experience that from any of my family members. When he set those boundaries with their mothers and communicated with me first instead of letting me find out about plans he had concerning the kids, it proved to me that I could trust that he valued my position in our marriage.

Boundaries can be set for in-laws too. Once you make that vow to leave and cleave, you must honor that. There may be times when certain people will try to make you feel bad for setting boundaries, but what's important is that three-strand cord – yourself, your spouse, and God. Make the decision respectfully but make it!

Now that we've overcome those things that broke us, the love flows so much more freely. My husband understands how to navigate our blended family effectively, and I follow his lead. Respecting him in other ways came more easily. During our time apart, he used it to build trust back with me by his actions. He did things that he said he was going to do without having any excuses attached to it. I knew beyond the shadow of a doubt that I was his first priority. He loved me and respected me as his wife more than before. I knew how much he'd always loved me. However, it was the respect and concern for my feelings that I didn't feel. When he made the suggestion to sell our home and purchase a bigger and better one, my ability to follow his lead came with much more ease. While we were divorced, Will had the opportunity to start a new career. He chose to really be the head of his household in every aspect. He put his family in a better position by starting a new career, so he would be able to provide for his family consistently. He found out through one of his friends about the opportunity to take courses and get certifications with FEMA. He jumped right on it! This happened around the time of the BP oil spill. I believe it was around 2009. We were newly divorced, and the tensions from our divorce were high. We were doing what we needed to do for the kids in a nutshell, but there was still a lot of blaming and arguing going on. We had tension overall about our decision to get divorced, which I wanted, but he didn't.

When he got the opportunity to change his career path, he did that, and with that career change, he landed a long-term contract with the BP oil spill down in Mississippi. In 2010, Will had a leadership position with FEMA. He wanted to show me that he had improved on some of the previous things that broke our marriage down in reference to finances. He made a great deal of money. Even though we had not remarried yet, he positioned himself strategically by allowing those paychecks to be deposited in my account, my personal checking account that we did not share jointly. He knew that he could trust me with his income. We were able to use those deposits to show proof of income on my behalf because our first and second homes that we had together were purchased solely in my name.

Because he brought his income to the table, I was able to obtain a loan to build a solid foundation and a better home for us and our growing family. The level of respect that I had for him for doing this skyrocketed. The fact that he put our family in position to have a solid foundation gave me feelings of such joy. This was the first time that he really had a stable income with a career that could support our family. It felt so good. I can see how hard he worked to not only provide for his family, but also he had a level of confidence as a man that suited him well. It was well deserved, and I was so proud of him. I loved and respected him.

2.0: Having respect in your marriage builds feelings of trust, safety, and well-being; this is key, and it is a foundation to having a healthy and passionate marriage. Respect and trust go hand in hand. Respect is something that is also necessary in a marriage. Once you and your spouse find a way to have mutual respect in every aspect of your marriage, you will see how much more easily the love will flow. Respect your spouse even when you're not in their presence. Oftentimes, when there is a heated argument between the husband and the wife, one spouse can find themselves venting to an outsider to have someone on their side. This type of behavior can paint a bad picture of that spouse that is oftentimes not true. This can be an ultimate form of disrespect because the other spouse is clueless as to what is being said behind their back. We believe you must keep respect at the forefront of your marriage. Some will even argue it's more important than love. Having respect in your marriage will help to ensure your needs and desires are met. This is the formula to building a healthy and passionate marriage.

Gracious Lord, please give my husband and me the blessings of living in a marriage that is highlighted in both honor and respect. May our responses to each other be punctuated with the spirit of love, so we consistently operate wholly and completely in an atmosphere that knows nothing other than respect. Help us keep respect at the forefront of our marriage. Amen.

℘

Love Happens Here.

Let's Get Back on Track!

What are the top three causes of communication breakdown in your marriage?

_____

_____

_____

_____

_____

_____

How would you like to see your spouse effectively communicate their needs and desires to you?

_____

_____

_____

_____

_____

_____

CHAPTER 4

Keep Calm

K eep calm. Sometimes, it's easier said than done. Refrain from being combative or undermining each other during conflict. Understand that each person is an individual, and effective communication can allow you to understand each other completely. Effective communication to us means that when talking with your spouse, you speak and then listen, but you listen to understand your spouse's concerns, needs, wants, and whatever may be bothering or angering them. Then, work together to find a solution to the problem. Effective communication is not listening to respond because a lot of times when we listen to respond, we respond in haste, and we respond only to get our point across. We are not listening to what our spouse is really asking of us or what they are saying they feel. Therefore, the argument continues, and it even blows up. In a marriage, you are still two individuals who come with your own mindset; it's okay to have a difference of opinion. Remember the love you have for each other and let that love take over by speaking kindly and reassure each other that you will work together to make the situation better. Your words should be followed by action.

Wilber speaking: One night while listening to Ed Sheeran's "Thinking Out Loud," I got into a mood, and I wanted to have a passionate night with my wife. I wanted to make love to her, and I got to the point where I wanted to tell her what I was thinking. If you haven't heard the Ed Sheeran song, "Thinking Out Loud", pull it up on your favorite music platform and listen to the first couple of verses. It's a really romantic song. It always reminded me of my wife. That night, it was already 11:00 p.m. I was downstairs relaxing in the lounge and having my night cap like I normally do when I listened to the song. I texted her, "Can you take your clothes off?" She replied, "Why?" This is the new-age of technology, and I guess in this new texting world, I read her one-word reply, and I got so upset. I really don't remember what happened after that, but I know we got into the biggest argument because I was in the mood, and I wanted her to be in the mood with me. When I read her response, "Why?", it went from 0 to 100. It's always best to keep calm. Don't get too caught up in the moment without getting a full understanding of why someone said or did something. Do you have a method that you use to diffuse disagreements in your marriage?

Quashaunda speaking: In total, Will and I have been married for over twenty years. That's a lifetime. During this time, we've had our fair share of disagreements, many of which have turned into arguments and sometimes blow ups, which really took a toll on our marriage. Thank God that these blow ups are a thing of the past. I honestly tried to block them out of my memory because they were so bad at times to the point that I don't want to remember the details of how they went down. However, for the purpose of this book and to help guide other married couples in a direction that will help them keep their marriage passionate and healthy, I'm going to recall some of these memories and let you guys know some of the things that we experienced.

We each have our own way of dealing with our disagreements. When a disagreement is turning into a full blow up, we have a method to defuse the situation quickly. Will likes to count down from ten mentally. It allows him to listen, and it allows me to get my point across. Then, we have a moment of silence to break the tension in the room. For me, I prefer to step away and calm my mind, so we can revisit the issue peacefully. When I say that I step away, I don't mean that I leave the house or anything. I might go into another room and listen to some calming music or do something that really calms my mind like cleaning.

I'm a neat freak, so a lot of times, I'll just take a break to clean, or I'll even take a break and work out in the basement in our gym. These things really calm me down and allow my mind to process so much. I am able to allow those thoughts to just flow out of my mind in a manner that I am able to think rationally without blowing up; both methods allow for a cooldown period. When we reconvene, we tend to find a solution even if we still have a difference of opinion. This is so important because, again, you have two individuals who have to come together in a marriage to build something beautiful. There will be differences of opinion, and that is totally okay. Being able to respect your spouse enough to understand they may think differently than you in one area doesn't make them love you any less. The love should still be there, and when you find a solution to your issue, you will see that the love only will build and grow much more.

Some of our fights got downright nasty, and I mean, downright ugly. We said things to each other that we should not have said. Name calling is the worst because even though time has

29

passed, those words are still in the mind of your spouse. That's not how we should conduct ourselves in a marriage. We found ourselves doing that time and time again. In this 2.0 marriage, we may have a conversation that leads to a disagreement, but it's refreshing to know that these disagreements won't turn into a blow up of the past.

We may have a difference of opinion or a misunderstanding, but we are able to reach a solution in which we still can talk to each other with respect and love each other. Then, we will be able to quickly move past whatever issue is concerning us. When the conversation starts to get heated, have an effective way to defuse the situation. A disagreement handled incorrectly will turn into an argument that leads to a bigger problem – disrespect. However, a disagreement handled with respect will turn into a conversation that will lead to changed behavior or a solution. There is a difference. Disagreements are acceptable. Disrespect is not. It is important that you listen to understand and not to respond. Practicing this will bring more peace and understanding in your marriage. You will be able to take each other's concerns to heart and find a solution, which will make your spouse not only feel loved but valued, and that is key to building and maintaining a healthy and passionate marriage.

CHAPTER 5

Own It!

O wn your mess! None of us are perfect. When you
know you have caused your spouse pain, either by your
actions or your words, take ownership. This is not the
time when you do something knowingly or unknowingly, and
you see how upset your spouse is, and you act as if you don't
know what happened. Recall Urkel's famous words, from the
highly rated sitcom *Family Matters*, and ask yourself that famous
question. Apologize. Apologize physically with a comforting
hug and a gentle kiss. Apologize verbally and acknowledge your
spouse's feelings and needs. Take the necessary actions to show
your spouse that you are working on changing or improving
your behavior in this area. Show your spouse that you know you
did something that bothered them. Give your spouse the space
they may need to process what has happened and allow them to
come back around. Now, you can't wait until Christmas to come
back around. However, when you have been the one to cause the
pain, you must take into account it may take longer than you

would like for your spouse to come back around. That's the risk you take when there are certain things that you may have done that ticked your spouse off. Make sure to iron these things out in conversations, so the distance created between you and your spouse can be shorter and shorter, even nonexistent.

Wilber speaking: Knowing I caused so much pain to my wife, Shaunda, I had to understand how to own up to my mistakes, my faults, and my errors. There were times when I would understand why she would be so upset. I would ask questions over and over just to try to get a full understanding of what her thought process was or what her next move might be. I also wanted to know if she would retaliate. This chapter will help you understand that by owning up to it, there are certain things you must do to give your spouse the space and time to heal. The hurt may be so deep to the point that both of you need time to figure out what is needed to better the situation. You have to figure out how each individual can show up better in the situation. There were times when I would look at situations only from my point of view, and I would tell my wife to get over it. I wanted her to let it go. Now that I know that pain is so deep, it's easier said than done. When I have caused her pain, I realize that I must allow her time. Whenever there's a situation in which she is hurt, I need to be able to give her her space. Maybe it is her meditation time, but if she's not giving me that affection or that attention, and the insecurities set in, I will feel lonely and neglected. I will feel like whatever I did was in vain, and I will be trying to figure out what the problem is when the problem was me all along. I caused the hurt, so now that I'm hurting, and she's hurting, it is not a good situation. That is not a good place in which to find yourself. We have to own it, which means we have to allow that person time to heal. We have to give them their space.

Quashaunda speaking: I'll be the first to say that my husband, Will, knows my love language. However, knowing my trigger points is something that we need to work on. Sometimes, I think he knows what triggers me, and he has pushed those buttons without wanting to own it. Because we've been able to work through our issues and have that respect for one another, even if there is a time that we mess up (that he messes up), he's taken ownership. That's what I love, and that's what I can appreciate. One of my trigger points is when people ask me the same question over and over, but in different ways, like the answer will change. I also don't like it when people don't pay attention. That really gets under my skin and gets my blood boiling. This causes me to have unnecessary stress. I'm the type of person that when I speak, I speak very clearly. I'll tell a story and go around in five circles just to make sure that I cover every single detail; I get so excited. My husband often says the tone of my voice is harsh. What do I do? I own it because I know that sometimes when I speak, I get so passionate about what I'm saying. I'm very detailed. Something people wouldn't guess about me is that I curse, and I curse a lot. With my passion, those curse words get offensive. It sounds like I'm yelling and complaining. Have you ever heard the saying, "Those sound like fighting words to me!"? This is what he hears. When I get that response from him, I know that I need to tone it down. I own it.

When I'm asked a question, and I give an answer, and then I'm asked a similar question about the same thing but in another way, and I give the same answer, and then I'm asked the same thing again, that gets under my skin. I immediately have to let my husband know, "Hey, this is starting to look like you're doing this to get under my skin, and I don't like it." Then, we will just come together. We really talk to each other about what it is that he wants to know. When he listens effectively, we'll both realize he understood what I said, and in the beginning, he just may not have been paying attention.

Knowing the trigger points and avoiding them at all costs will help to keep the marriage healthy and the passion flowing, so the next time you feel heated, think back on those practices that will diffuse the situation and put them into play. Blatant disrespect can not only be hurtful to your spouse, but it also can cause stress and anxiety. Understand that each person is an individual with their own opinions. There will be times you two will have a difference of opinion. During conflict, effective communication can allow for complete understanding. Be sure to refrain from expecting a response before communicating.

Every marriage consists of two individuals at different stages of awareness. To grow together, you must be willing to work together, which includes anything that is unhealed within. This is how your marriage elevates. Your spouse is an individual, so during their healing time, take time to work on yourself and see how this will increase the respect your spouse has for you. Again, allow your spouse time to heal. Mutual respect is a simple concept. It means to treat your spouse in a thoughtful and courteous manner. I like to live by the scripture, Matthew 7:12. It says, "So in everything, do to others what you would have them do to you."

CHAPTER 6

A Solid Foundation

Trust comes after there is some level of respect. The importance of trust in your marriage will allow you to be more open and giving to your spouse. Trust in a marriage is the belief in your spouse, and respect is that trust in action. You can see how these two are deeply intertwined, and when they are executed properly, it can lead to a healthy and passionate marriage. Ephesians 5:33 says, "However, each one of you also must love his wife as he loves himself, and the wife must respect her husband."

Wilber speaking: Brick by brick. That's the only way to build a solid foundation in your marriage. You must have a solid foundation in order to have a healthy and passionate marriage. The foundation has to consist of love, trust, and respect. Because a man is supposed to be the provider, you need to make sure your financial situation is solid. It's a must. Fellas, it's not something that you can overlook. You must establish a solid foundation that's built from healthy love, trust, respect, and finances. It may sound cliché, but you can't have a foundation without having these things in order. However, a lot of times, men tend to be missing one or more of these bricks, which are principles, to ensure our foundation is solid. This is of vital importance because once one of them goes missing, there's a lack of trust that will result. Let's say in my case, throughout my first marriage, there were times when my financial situation was not the best. I would go from job to job, business to business, and hustle to hustle. I was just trying to figure it out. Although I kept trying, it just wouldn't pan out in my favor. I would chase other people's dreams with them. I did not realize that I had dreams of my own to build, and when you have a wife who is working with you, you can build an empire! That should have been the main focus. I should have been focusing on my own strengths and skills. I should have been finding a career or passion and nurturing it to provide for my family and build a solid foundation for us. When you're young, you're just trying to figure life out. You're trying to go with whatever you feel is going to bring you cash instead of really setting yourself up for the future for financial freedom. To each his own, but college is not for everybody. Study yourself to know your strengths and get into a career or get some certifications that will allow you to provide for yourself and your family. Get something that always will keep you employed or start your own business.

Entrepreneurship is hard work so make sure you position your business correctly, so you can have a successful one. Practice discipline with your finances, so they will grow more and not decline. Do your homework, so your finances are in order. You also need that trust from your wife beyond the shadow of a doubt, so she will know you won't do anything to hurt her and break her trust in you. That's what I tell a lot of my friends. They said, "Man, you've been married for twenty-plus years. You got married in 1999. What do I need to do man? What do I need to do?" I tell them the number one thing. Don't hurt your wife. Don't hurt your girl. Don't bring that drama to her, to the house, or to your place of peace. Keep the pain away from your wife. This way, you keep the butterflies feeling in her stomach. She still will feel that passionate lovey-dovey feeling. This is how you keep her trust in you. Show your wife through your actions that you are the best man and husband for her. However, if there's an inkling of a doubt, then that trust goes out the window. It's hard to build a solid foundation when there's something missing, especially trust. Trust is one of the most important aspects, if not the foundation, of a healthy marriage. In marriages, the stability of your foundation is critical for a peaceful and successful marriage. This is built, maintained, and nurtured by both spouses daily.

Quashaunda speaking: This time around in our marriage, the respect my husband earned allowed me to trust that his past mistakes and boundaries that were crossed in our first marriage would not show up in this marriage. To have that feeling means that I can love more freely without reservation, and the passion will flow. In our first marriage, we dealt with the consequences of, not necessarily infidelity, but a trust factor in the way I found out about his other relationships. A more fitting word would be "situationships" that led to his other children outside of our marriage. There were two kids my husband had already before we got married. When he had his first child, we were not dating yet. While the mother was pregnant with his first daughter, I specifically asked the question, "Do you have any kids?" He said, "No." That "no" was a bit tricky because at the time, he honestly did not know the mother was still pregnant with his child. He thought that the pregnancy had been terminated because of what he and the mother had previously agreed. However, that was not the case. When he found out, his daughter had already been born. Nevertheless, when he found out that she was born, I'm sure all sorts of thoughts ran through his mind.

In a nutshell, this was not what I wanted in my life. With that being said, the way I found out was devastating. It was maybe a month after he initially found out. We had been dating for a year when I got the news. I remember that night and conversation so well. He was very short with his words. Feelings and emotions were very high. I had just terminated our pregnancy because we agreed that we were not ready to be parents, so to hear the news of him having a child was absolutely soul crushing. That type of hurt I wish on no one. My trust was shattered into a million pieces, and it seemed like it might take a lifetime to put it back together. Now, it did take a long time, but thank God it didn't take a lifetime.

Even when your spouse has lost trust in you, they still love you. They want to have the trust back that they once gave so freely. Not only does it benefit you to know your spouse trusts you. It also benefits them and allows them to feel safe to love you with passion and vulnerability. Trust is a two-way street. The easiest way to say it is don't do something that would disappoint you if you discovered your spouse was doing it. Realizing that your actions played a part in your spouse's distrust is the first step to resolving the issue. Be honest and open about your feelings. This is the time to let it all out, so there can be healing, and you can set boundaries. Be patient with your spouse. Don't force it by expecting them to trust you completely so soon. Give it time. Show your spouse how much you love and care for them, keeping the need to regain their trust as your top priority. Doing this reassures your spouse that you are willing to do what it takes to regain their trust, and you will feel the trust coming back into your marriage.

In our first marriage, the trust was broken in more than one instance. Due to the instability of my husband's income, it was hard for me to trust that he was able to provide for our family. This caused me to stress over life's basic needs, which depleted the passion I desired to have in our marriage. We were always working, trying to make ends meet. We were robbing Peter to pay Paul to the point that we had a routine. We look back on it now, and we laugh; it really was not a bad routine, but it was something that became a very integral part of our marriage to make sure that we didn't really miss a beat. Most times, the finances were very tight. We had to live on a strict budget. For example, I worked in the early 2000s, and we got married in 1999. My cooking skills were nowhere near what they are now. However, as a good wife and good mother, you make sure that your family never goes hungry. Our meal of choice was Hamburger Helper. We had Hamburger Helper every possible way. We had every flavor. These days, I will not even look at Hamburger Helper! When I walk down the aisle in the grocery store, I don't even want to look at it. I don't want to bring back haunted memories because we ate so much.

On Thursdays, we would have Pizza Hut to be exact – pepperoni pizza, meat lovers, pan crust, with extra cheese. We had it every Thursday or every other Thursday like clockwork. How do I know? We would be so tight on funds. They were running low by Thursday. I would write a check. Back then, the technology wasn't as great, so you actually had to take the check to the bank and deposit it before those funds would clear. That gave me time to write a check on Thursday night, knowing that my direct deposit would hit on Friday morning. By the time the employees took the check into the bank on Friday to clear the check for that Pizza Hut dinner, we would be in the clear. We had a system like clockwork. I wish I still had those canceled checks.

Those were some of the things in our first marriage that we had to work through. I was always trying to figure out a way to make it through our financial challenges because I had a stable income. Will did a lot of gigs back in the day. When he didn't have a gig, he would have a 9-5 job, but those jobs would be short-lived. There was a lot of stress having to think about how we were going to eat, how we were going to pay the bills, and how we were going to do this or that. It really took a toll on us, and it depleted the passion I desired to have in our marriage. However, during our time apart, my ex-husband, at the time, knew how important stability was for me. He knew the struggles that we had in the past, and he knew that was something I could not deal with in this marriage 2.0. Having a steady and great income to support our family allowed me to regain trust for him in this area and in other areas. He really ramped up his career, taking classes with OSHA, and he got certifications, so he can work on natural disasters. Granted, this career path takes him out of town quite often, but now we're at a place where we are very much more stable, and he's able to come home a lot when he's working out of town.

I appreciate the fact that he took that into consideration. That was one of the main things that tore our marriage apart the first time, so he wanted to make sure that this time around, he got it right. I truly, truly appreciate that, and the love and passion is there, so it was easier for me to follow his lead. Not only did I want and need to trust my husband, but I also had to trust myself in knowing that I was making the right decision for myself concerning us getting remarried. My husband's words and actions allowed me to regain the trust I had for him. For a person who broke the trust of your spouse, it can feel like you're walking on eggshells. However, staying true to your word not only alleviates these feelings, but it also brings reassurance to your spouse.

Most marriages are new to both parties involved. While there is a fairytale-type of love that exists, there is also room for trust to be broken. This is often not done intentionally. Don't blame yourself or live in the past about mistakes that you made. Communicate, learn from them, and open your heart back up to trust again. Trust is *key* to having a healthy and passionate marriage.

Dear God, thank you for my marriage, despite what my husband and I have been through. I pray that we always will be willing to show trust in our marriage. I want to trust my husband fully. However, I know there are areas of my heart that cause me to hang on to the past. Cleanse my heart and renew my mind, so these things may truly be a thing of the past, and love and passion will continue to flow in our marriage. In Jesus's name we pray, Amen.

∽

Love Happens Here.

Let's Get Back on Track!

In order of importance what are the top three goals you want to accomplish to have the healthy and passionate marriage that you desire?

_____

_____

_____

_____

_____

List three ways that you can show respect to your spouse by creating healthy boundaries.

_____

_____

_____

_____

_____

_____

CHAPTER 7

Regain the Trust

Once trust has been broken, use trust building exercises to regain it. Part of rebuilding trust is being trustworthy. Make sure your spouse knows that without a shadow of a doubt, they can trust you, especially in areas that the trust was broken in the past. In this area of regaining trust, we have to be self-aware. Make sure we check ourselves before doing or saying something that may have caused hurt in the past. Thinking about the outcome beforehand will give you the opportunity to self-correct before the situation gets out of hand. This will help to build and maintain the healthy and passionate marriage that you both desire. Trust that your spouse wants to gain your trust back, and they have your best interest at heart. Love your spouse in a way that shows you can be trusted. This can be done by keeping your word and doing the things you said you would do. Do the small things that you know your spouse likes. This can be done with everyday routine things. We make an attempt every day to keep our marriage healthy. My husband starts the day off with a beautiful prayer. Because he mainly works away from home, he texts me beautiful prayers every morning about our marriage and its growth – present and future.

Wilber speaking: Part of getting my day off to a great start is hearing my wife's voice. However, my career requires me to wake up at the crack of dawn while she's still sound asleep, or I'm working away from home. My wife knows that although I've been working for about two hours before she wakes up, I'm patiently waiting on her call. Those morning phone calls I get after I've gotten my day started are important to me. It shows that my wife understands that this is one way I view trust. However, when I see that she's already been on social media while she is on her throne, I feel slighted. This is something that we've discussed on more than one occasion. Each time, we get more and more in tune about why this is important to me as her husband. It not only establishes the trust in our marriage, but it also shows that she respects my concern. It shows that I care for her, and I care for our family and their well-being. She understands my position as the protector of our family, and she knows the peace this brings me.

I have to channel my feelings and let them stay positive. My intention is to show her that I trust her, and I do not want to be controlling and then have accusations to follow. When we haven't healed ourselves yet, we can find that we are being controlling, and we can accuse our spouse of what we did in the past. Not only do I want to just hear her voice to make my day, but I also want to hear her voice to make sure that she's off to a great start. I want to know that she and my daughter are going to have a great day, and I can speak words of affirmation and love over her and our daughter, making sure they both get their day off to a great start. We're all busy with day-to-day activities, careers, family, and social engagement. However, be sure to keep your commitment to your spouse as a top priority. This will help you regain trust in your marriage, especially during those times when you are rebuilding trust. This is key to making sure the marriage stays healthy and passionate.

No one wants to be in a marriage in which they feel they can't trust their spouse beyond where they can see them or as they say, "I can't trust you as far as I can throw you." Make sure you're keeping your spouse's needs, wants, and desire to feel secure as your top priorities in your marriage. Remember, when you are faced with difficult situations, speak what you want, not what you don't want. Tell your spouse how their actions can help you regain your trust in them. Stay away from being controlling and stay positive.

If I told you guys that I was perfect, I would be telling you something far from the truth. I'm not perfect. Who is? There have been times that I have broken my wife's trust. I have caused our marriage some real pain. I am honored she gave me another chance to get it right. I'm grateful to God that He gave us another chance. He strengthened me in the ways that I needed to be strengthened, so if and when I was given the opportunity to get my family back, I would be ready.

In this chapter, I'm going to go deep and tell you what I had to work through to get where I needed to be not only in my marriage but with myself as well. I hope that this will help the husbands reading this to understand how to regain your wife's trust regarding this situation. Sometimes, husbands make their wives feel less than sexually like they're unable to satisfy their husbands' sexual appetite. In most cases, it's not her at all. Better yet, I pray that you have not had to go through this because this can be a hard one to bounce back from. I pray that you take this one to heart. Words to the wise from Chris Tucker aka

Smokey in the hit movie *Friday*, about what not to do. FUCK!"
Just don't do it!!!

One thing I did was get my thought process in order. I had
to get my vices and the things that were entertaining to me
under control. It was a real mindset shift. You have to get those
things in control, whether it's the strip club, social media, or
spending too much time away from home just hanging with
the guys. Fellas, we have a man code. *Relax.* I'm not giving
away the code; however, for the purpose of understanding my
point, here's an example. We have things that we do. If it's a
nice old school car, we might share it via our phone, or if it's an
attractive female model, a lot of guys have different group chats
where we share those things. To be honest, it's not necessarily a
bad thing. We're human. Men are visual hunters and pursuers.
Where the problem lies is when those things get out of control.
How do you know when it's gotten out of control? Well, the
visually pleasing images of other women cause strife in your
marriage, unknowingly, because you're looking at something
appealing to the eye, or you are attracted to it. Then, you come
home, trying to figure out why your wife is not satisfying this
feeling that you have. That isn't fair because she doesn't know
what you have been looking at all day long.

You have to allow yourself time away from those things that
are appealing to you and are taking you away from what your
wife brings to the table – the realness of love, her softness, and
her caring and loving spirit. You love the way she manages your
household to make sure everyone's needs are met – the kids' needs
and your needs. Sometimes, we're unaware that we are the ones
causing more strife in our marriage by using outside influences
as a way of getting aroused or liking the pictures or watching
certain things that are sexual to us. I would sometimes get into
trouble with social media posts, looking at them a little too much.

First, I had to realize this indeed was a problem. It was causing irritation to my wife, and even though it may still appeal to my senses, I do not want to hurt my wife. I do not want to be the reason for strife in our marriage. Instead, I only want to love her and bring her joy and peace. I want to let her know that she could and very much does satisfy my sexual desires. I had to fall back from that and eliminate the minutes that turned into hours watching images and videos on my phone of other women. Secondly, I had to become consistent in what I wanted in my marriage. I had to become a better version of myself. One thing I started doing on a daily basis was praying. I began to pray for God to heal me in this way and other ways. I began praying an intentional and detailed prayer for my marriage. I prayed for my family and for everything that I wanted God to heal. I sent these text messages to my wife every day to show her where my mindset is now versus where it was when I was causing her pain. Your mindset has to shift into what you want in your marriage, and more importantly, you have to act on it.

That was one way of acting on what I wanted in our marriage. I was being consistent, staying disciplined, and at the same time, showing my wife that I'm getting closer to God; I also was getting closer to the way that I should be. I was moving away from all those things that were causing problems, not realizing they were causing problems. Because from general conversations and just being in society, it seems like most men are sex addicts. We are addicted to sex. It's everywhere in music, commercials, movies, tv shows, and shopping. We think about it all day, and we look at pictures all day. We watch pornography, and then we come home trying to figure out how and why our wives don't arouse us in that way when they have their day-to-day activities to deal with. They are running multiple businesses, organizing our daughters' activities, and building school brands.

Nowadays, women wear a lot of hats, and we're trying to figure out how to get aroused all the time when it's just impossible because it's in our face 24/7. Take ownership and realize the hurt that this could be causing in your marriage. You've got to scale back and have this conversation with your wife, so she's able to understand that you need and desire for her to make time for you as well. Let your wife be sexy on her terms. Don't try to do it forcibly. Allowing her to come to you in that way can be a game changer. Reignite that fire and experience the passion in your marriage, specifically your bedroom. As the Bible says in Hebrews 13:4, **(NKJV)**, "Marriage is honorable among all and the bed undefiled; fornicators and adulterers God will judge."

Quashaunda speaking: As the spouse on the receiving end of having your trust broken, the decision to trust your spouse again can feel impossible. You run through different scenarios over and over again, playing them out in detail in your head. Though you may feel like you're getting the answers you want by drawing your own conclusion, you're really just delaying the process of healing to regain trust. Yes, it may be easier said than done. After all, you're the one who was betrayed. However, once you've really and wholeheartedly made the decision to forgive and trust again, you've gotten one step closer to coming out on the other side.

Trust does not always have to do with infidelity. Other reasons may be not following through on a promise, not taking responsibility for inexcusable behavior, or withholding love or affection as a form of punishment. When your spouse is emotionally unavailable, it can leave you feeling lonely and neglected. Your spouse may have had an emotional (nonsexual) affair. Your spouse may have addictive behaviors such as drugs, alcohol, pornography, and gambling. Your spouse may break your trust by directly criticizing you or speaking badly about you behind your back, especially to family members.

In spite of the terrible damage these actions may cause, rebuilding trust is very possible. Seek God first and ask Him to come in the midst of your marriage and start to heal your heart. The next step is that both of you must be willing to work on the marriage, and the main goal should be to rebuild a sense of safety. You must allow the injured spouse time to make a knowledgeable decision about how to rebuild trust and whether they want to proceed in the marriage. However, this takes time, and rushing or pressuring your spouse to hurry up and decide will only make matters worse. You have to understand their mental state at this point. In most cases, it can feel like their entire world has been shattered. They may have to seek therapy first to even cope or think rationally about the two of you as a married couple so give it time. Once this is achieved, the decision to forgive needs to be made. Now this doesn't mean that they will forget the damage that has been done. However, making the decision to forgive means they no longer let it control their emotions, and when it does come back to the forefront of their mind, you BOTH work on a set of principles that you develop together to move forward in a positive and healthy direction. Refrain from being an investigator of your spouse, questioning their every move and being defensive in every situation. This will help to strengthen your emotional muscles. As the injurer, be willing to answer simple questions about the betrayal so a more destructive image isn't created, and the pressure to know more is alleviated. Both parties must want to work on the marriage. In the case of infidelity, one spouse shares all unavoidable encounters with whom the affair happened. This can be a challenge if the other person is a coworker or the biological parent of their child. In all honesty, any encounters need to be avoided completely!

When you see that your spouse is making an honest attempt to repair the damage, accept it and move forward. Get it out! Have a truthful talk about the betrayal. Set aside time to talk about what happened. Don't drag it out. Make it a short fifteen to twenty minute conversation. Make an outline beforehand, if necessary, to stay on track. Evaluate your progress weekly, and as you see improvements, start to decrease the frequency of your meetings. Develop some healthy boundaries together to eliminate the possibility of the betrayal happening again. Lastly, develop an appreciation system when progress is being made. Show it by performing your spouse's love language. This can help to reignite the passion back into your marriage.

Rebuilding the trust in your marriage will take time, commitment, a willingness to forgive, and a continual effort to prioritize your marriage. The healthy and passionate marriage that you stand to gain will far exceed your investment. Again, both partners must participate actively in rebuilding the trust in your marriage. The above-mentioned principles provide a simple and effective guide to build and maintain a healthy and passionate marriage.

Lord, have mercy on our marriage and rebuild the trust and honesty that has escaped our marriage. Lord, I want our marriage to be healed. Let the healing begin with me. Have mercy on me, Oh Lord. As a spouse who has failed to demonstrate Your love, help me to be a vessel of Your love, peace, faithfulness, patience, goodness, and self-control in my spouse's life. Remove and break all ungodly soul-ties. Lord, let healing take place. Let deliverance take place. Let joy take place. Let peace abide in us. Lord, I command a seven-fold restoration of the trust, honesty, and love that has been stolen from us in Jesus's name. Amen.

CHAPTER 8

Distinguish Between Trust and Control

E arly on in your marriage, distinguish how trust and control looks to you. If you are not careful, these lines can cross easily. This is a slippery slope that can show up in a marriage quite often when there is a lack of effective communication. This becomes more prevalent when there has been an abuse of trust in a marriage in the past. Have you ever heard of the term, "millennial marriage"? Of course, we have. It's everywhere. They have websites about it. There are articles about it. They're hashtags on social media and social media pages dedicated to it. Everybody is talking about a millennial marriage. What does that actually mean? Well, in a nutshell, a millennial marriage is, as you can guess, different from some of our parents' marriages, and it definitely is different from our grandparents and great grandparents.

All in all, I enjoy the freedom of a millennial marriage. However some of the values of older, strict-belief marriages are a necessity.

We have more freedom as individuals and together as a couple in a millennial marriage. Some of the benefits are that you are more open to economic roles, meaning sometimes, the bread-winner is not always the husband. Back in the day, that would not exist. The women were taught to cook, clean, and raise the children. For those who find love outside of their race, it's more acceptable now than it has been in the past. Also, it's okay to have kids later on in life, which is something that I really appreciate. I just could not fathom having a child in the eighth or ninth grade when you're only thirteen or fourteen years old, like some of my great aunts. The decision to start having kids in my twenties and finish at thirty-four is something that I'm able to handle much better. On the flip side, millennial marriages come with some of the challenges that elders did not have to experience. One of the main ones we're going to discuss in this chapter are those tiny heavyweight devices also known as cell phones.

Quashaunda speaking: Cell phones, cell phones, cell phones. We can't live with them, and we can't live without them. These lightweight, small devices carry an enormous amount of information about a person. Think about it. Take a minute and think about how often you use your cell phone and what you use it to do. You use it for business, entertainment, personal information, family member information, important dates, banking investments, and the list can go on. You can see how one may get lost in it. If you steal a person's cell phone, you can easily steal their identity. You literally have their life in the palm of your hands.

My husband is a real people's person, and oftentimes, he gets lost spending time on his cell phone, as we all do at times.

However, in the past, there has been some questionable information in his cell phone. Yeah, I did what most people say you shouldn't do, but when I have an intuition, I go with it. Therefore, I did go through his phone.

When I did, I saw some things that I didn't like. I saw that he was sending and receiving different images and videos of women and things of that sort on his phone. At that moment, we sat down to have the conversation and distinguish between trust and control. We developed some clear boundaries that worked for us to navigate through that situation. It's necessary in your marriage that when conflict comes, you have a plan to set boundaries in certain situations to change behaviors and make improvements. This will help you to build a healthy marriage. It's not that I wanted to be in control, but because of his actions, there was a lack of trust. That led me to take the device, go through it, and see some questionable things that we had to work through, and we did work through these issues by doing some of the same practices we listed here in this chapter.

With that behind us, we have an understanding. I have an understanding of some things he may have been feeling or experiencing. He has a better understanding of how I feel about the situation and what are some things I go through day to day that impacted why I was not showing up in an area where he may have wanted me to show up. Once we worked through those issues and got to the bottom of the issues, that created a space for us to have healthy communication. Because of that healthy communication and the actions we took to move forward in a positive direction, we were able to reignite, even more passionately on a deeper level in our marriage. I'm making an effort to trust that the past is the past, and I do not want to be controlling anymore. Although I do see him on his phone, I can now be at ease. They hold a lot of information and are very entertaining, even necessary.

Even if he's on the phone, I have to be self-aware and at peace, knowing that he's doing just as he says he's doing. He's not trying to hurt me again. We're not going back into the past. We've learned from it. Together, we set boundaries, and we are moving forward. I trust that what he said he's doing on the phone is what he actually is doing on the phone. That also gives me peace to let it go. I have peace to not let that consume me and take away from the passion that I want to give to the marriage because we've already addressed it. During our second time around, we've made sure that we're not going back into the past. We made sure that we're not hurting each other in ways that we know to be hurtful already. Dealing with past hurt in your marriage definitely can cause trust issues that can lead to a controlling spouse. You have to make up your mind that you know that your spouse is not there to hurt you, and you have ironed out all those issues. You must determine that you're going to move forward in a positive direction because you want to stay happily married.

The biggest part of having trust in your marriage is being trustworthy. Most times, a lack of trust can turn into control issues that stem from your own insecurities. If not addressed, these will show up in your marriage in a number of ways. This is why healing is so important. No matter what happened in your past relationships before this marriage or with past situations in the marriage that you're in now, you have to take time and heal from those situations. Everyone talks about healing. What does that mean? Healing looks different for everyone, but it's vital for everyone. Everyone is responsible for their own healing. Now, you and your spouse can support each other while you heal; however, the decision is yours. You have to make the decision and take the necessary action to change your behavior. You need to be a better you and a healed and whole you. Showing up whole in your marriage creates a safe space for your love to thrive.

Keep this as top priority. When you do this, you'll see it's not a thing of control. You are making sure your spouse feels safe and secure in your marriage.

Wilber speaking: It's Friday, and as a highly sought-after esthetician in Metro Atlanta, I know my wife is busy with clients at her business. However, the need for me to speak to her is my top priority at the moment. I call and text her repeatedly. My wife, on the other hand, is hard at work and livid with these, in her mind, non-important phone calls and text messages. The need for me to speak to her at that moment, knowing it's not an emergency, is being controlling and showing a lack of trust. I had to check myself really quickly. I was letting past hurts come back into my mind, and they were trying to control my thoughts. I also was allowing my guilty conscience to play a part in the controlling demeanor I was having at the time. However, because I self-corrected and stopped the back-to-back calls, once we finally got on the phone, I initiated a pleasant conversation instead of one filled with accusations and yelling. She went on to explain how busy her day was with work (which I knew already). The conversation was peaceful and refreshing, which in turn made our evening filled with passion, the way we really wanted it to be after a long week. Fellas, if this ever happens to you, first realize what's happening and make the adjustment quickly. Failure to do so can lead to old feelings of betrayal coming back up from your spouse, and that surely will take you backwards. When you're in a healing process, the goal is to move forward to build a healthy and passionate marriage.

Solid marriages have to be built on trust. When you are regaining the trust back in your marriage, focus on the positives of the situation. Lead by example. Speak and do the things that you would want done for you, the way you know your spouse needs for reassurance. Make sure your spouse knows without a shadow of a doubt they can trust you, especially in areas that the trust was broken in the past. This will help to build and maintain the healthy and passionate marriage that you both desire. Refrain from controlling behavior, both verbally and physically. Instead, communicate effectively by asking direct questions, so you can get an honest and direct answer, eliminating doubt and the need to assume things. This will leave you with a sense of peace and reassurance of your spouse's love and respect for you.

Lord, I pray for our hearts to be healed, renewed, and restored. Help us to trust one another. Give us confidence in our spouse. Whether it is being loyal and faithful, getting something done, or being intimate, whatever the situation is, help us to trust each other. Help us to trust and love freely and with vulnerability. In Your name, we pray. Amen.

CHAPTER 9

All In

N ow that you have the fundamentals for a healthy marriage, and you are keeping God in the center of your marriage, while you are respecting and trusting each other, setting boundaries with co-parents and your in-laws, and establishing a solid foundation, you're ready to open your heart back up to love. Yes, you've loved your spouse all along. However, opening your heart back up to the person who hurt you can be a scary thing. Once you've made the decision to trust your spouse again, you have to forgive them. You don't have to forget what happened, but you have to forgive them, so you can love again. Forgive them, so you will be able to heal. Forgive them, so you will be able to move forward in a positive direction. Forgiveness puts you in a position to be able to give and receive love freely without conditions. That true unconditional love feels so much better. If you don't forgive your spouse, the hurt and anger you feel will consume you. Trust that your spouse knows the hurt they've caused and believe that they won't do it again. On the same note, if you're the one who abused your spouse's trust, then the choice to not abuse their trust again by repeating those same mistakes must be made.

Wilber speaking: When I say two people can be connected, I truly believe that because my wife and I had been separated for three years in total. We separated and went through a divorce. The divorce decree was final. We took all those steps. We stayed cordial for the kids, but I still felt connected to her even though she dated other people. I dated other people. We had things going on there, separately, but we were still connected. One day, I was on Moreland Avenue at the pool hall, which was maybe ten to fifteen minutes away from her apartment. If you know Atlanta, you know Moreland Avenue leads into Cleveland Avenue, and she had an apartment on Cleveland Avenue. On that day, while I was shooting pool, I got a knot in my stomach. I don't know where it came from. I know now it was probably God talking to me. That's my faith. When I got the knot, I sat down, and something told me to call Shaunda. When I heard her voice, I knew something was wrong. I can't remember how I asked what's wrong. All I know is I said, "Are you home?" She replied, "Yes," and I said, "I'm on the way!"

When I got to her apartment, she was distraught. I could see then what it was that I heard on the phone. She was upset about losing a client and friend of hers. During that time of bereavement, I was there to console her and be there for her. It was so ironic that in her moment of distress and feeling down, something hit me to the point I felt pain. I didn't know where it was coming from, but something told me to call her, and at that particular time, we started to rekindle our relationship. That's the time we started to get back together, and it felt good. It felt different. I was able to be there for her to help her go through a hard time she was experiencing. I felt my prayers had been answered. God answers our prayers, not necessarily when we want them, but when we're ready for them. This time, I was ready! I was ready to go "All In," giving my wife the trust, love, respect, and emotional and financial support I knew she needed and deserved from me as a husband.

Quashaunda speaking: I still have my journal where I wrote on January 22, 2010, "Met my homegirl at Cafe Circa. This loneliness cuts like a knife. I miss him.♥" After our divorce, I too became somewhat of a party girl – nothing wild or crazy. I hung out with friends and partied as a single woman. I dated. Some were good, and some were bad, but something, "that thing," was missing. I missed the peace I felt with him and the love we shared. I missed the way we complimented each other from the words we spoke. I missed completing each other's sentences to our actions of knowing what each other needed or wanted. These beautiful things had been minimized to being almost nonexistent due to the issues we had that were weighing so heavily in our marriage. However, it was this feeling that my mind and body were craving, and I couldn't find it anywhere or with anyone else. Exactly thirty one days later to the date, February 22, 2010, was the night he just spoke of when I had the honor of giving one last request to a friend. Wow! In 2022, twelve years later at this very moment of writing this, I now see the significance of those dates. God's timing is perfect. This is my confirmation. I'm a numbers person. The number twenty-two is also a master number, which means it has spiritual power, a sign of positive things to come. It is said to be the most powerful number of all. Twenty-two is often found to be linked to people who are doers, leaders, and visionary builders. These are individuals who are capable of turning wild dreams into solid accomplishments, blessed with the intuition of the number eleven but possessing a more disciplined approach to action. Whew! I'll take it.

Let's get back to the night that was mentioned previously. I remember it clearly. I had been home for a few hours after a long and emotional day. A client turned friend had passed away suddenly, and it was a shock to everyone. She was well-known and beloved in her community. She was only in her thirties. She passed from a heart attack in her sleep. Her infectious energy is what blossomed our client service-provider relationship into more of a friendship. She was feeling more positive about her newfound look, which I was a part of as her brow lady and makeup artist. When she unexpectedly passed away, her best friend with whom she always came to the salon asked me to do the honors of glamming her one last time. Her friend expressed how great and beautiful my client/friend felt when she left the salon after getting her hair and makeup done. I couldn't say no. I was nervous, scared, and honored. I felt all these emotions while I did her makeup, and she looked amazing.

When I got home, I was exhausted with those same feelings. As I sat on my couch while the boys were sleeping, I was trying to calm my nerves. That's when I got the phone call.

At that time, Will and I were cordial. The conversations were to the point, and they were mainly about the boys. There was nothing nasty about our communication, and there was no bickering. We just kept our boys at the forefront. When he called that late at night, I was shocked because the boys clearly didn't need anything. However, I was so happy because I knew he would be able to comfort me in a way that I needed. He gave me that reassurance that everything would be okay. He just held me while I cried because I had never experienced that before. He knew exactly what to say and do. When he called and asked if I was okay, and I told him that I wasn't, and he told me that he was on the way, I knew that it was the "something" I had been missing. He understood me and literally felt my pain. In the midst of the unfortunate and devastating circumstances, this was a beautiful moment.

I knew what we had was different, and if we took advantage of God's timing, this time it would be so much better. This was the beginning of our second time around. We both had decided to go "All In." The butterfly feeling was back like when we started dating in high school, not in a fairytale style. We had the reassurance that it was us and God and no one else. I remember an instance that happened when we first started dating after high school. We weren't seriously dating at that time. I had a date with a popular guy; however, I wished I was on a date with Wilber. In the middle of our date, I received a beeper message from Will. That feeling I got at the moment was pure bliss. I came up with some reason to end the date, so he would take me home. He did, and within an hour, I was where I wanted to be. I was on a date with my now husband. Similarly, before our second time around when we were dating, I was on another date. This time I wasn't rude, lol! The date was actually over. However, Will and I had been conversing earlier, and we both already had plans, but we were looking forward to seeing each other and spending time together.

This space we were in felt so peaceful. There was no pressure or drama. There was just love and forgiveness of what had been, and we were looking forward to what was to come. Our communication was healthy. We were in position, and we were willing to do the work together to build the healthy and passionate marriage we desired. The beauty is that this feeling is still here. Therefore, I'll say it's more than a feeling. It's our life, our love, and our respect for one another.

In our 2.0 marriage (second marriage to each other), we've had some amazing highs! One of our highs was the purchase of our dream home together. This is not our first home, but it was the first time we both had equal parts in the purchase of our home. It was one that we both loved and designed together. Because we made the sacrifices to put ourselves in a better financial position individually, we became stronger together, and we were able to purchase our dream home. Watching this process unfold before our eyes was evidence of the love we had for one another. We knew the part we both played in turning this dream into reality. The process took nine long months. The fact that we both put our family in position to generate wealth and create beautiful memories is a wonderful thing that makes us proud. We definitely see God's hand at work in our life.

Our life still has the everyday routine of married life, but it's beautiful because we've worked through all our issues, so even the routine of it all is what we love. We are married to someone we know has our back. We support each other in all aspects of our marriage. We do this in the best way we can. When you give from your heart, your spouse will feel it, accept it, and appreciate it. Just being able to be a place of peace for your spouse and vice versa will make you feel safe and respected in your marriage. You can do this by checking in with your spouse throughout the day or mainly when you get home. Genuinely ask about their day, so either way, good or bad, they'll feel supported enough by you to just let it all out. We also take time to enjoy what we've built with our home. We love to entertain our family and friends. Travel is also important to us with both our children, and of course, we love those vacations where it's just the two of us. For every couple, this may be different. Find what it is that you both enjoy doing together and then incorporate it into your marriage, so it can be your lifestyle and create the passion you desire to have in your marriage.

Marriage is about compromise and working together to achieve a desired goal. When the husband and wife work actively at this goal, success is achieved. Carve out consistent time in your schedule monthly or quarterly where you revisit your budget and financial goals to make sure you're still on the same page. When you make a plan together and hold each other accountable, it creates a stronger foundation and lessens your chance of being a statistic because your marriage fell apart due to finances. While you are taking care of the business side of your marriage, don't neglect the fun side, the side that brings you two closer. That feeling of being in love with your spouse is one of the greatest spaces in which you can find yourself.

"Love is patient, love is kind. It does not envy, it does not boast, it is not proud. It does not dishonor others, it is not self-seeking, it is not easily angered, it keeps no record of wrongs. Love does not delight in evil but rejoices with the truth. It always protects, always trusts, always hopes, always perseveres. Love never fails." 1 Corinthians 13:4-8

∽

Love Happens Here.

Let's Get Back on Track!

What are some things that may be holding you back from fully and passionately loving your spouse?

_____

_____

_____

_____

_____

Love language – acts of service, words of affirmation, physical touch, quality time and gifts. Each represent a unique way to express love. List some examples of how you show your spouse these love languages.

_____

_____

_____

_____

_____

CHAPTER 10

Love Language

" **I** love you" is said so often and very quickly. For instance, people say it when they are leaving home in the morning to start their day. It can be your salutation before getting off the phone, or you may type it in text messages. "I love you" is so common. However, how often do we actually slow down and take the time to show it? How often do we show it in a way that our spouse will feel it? That's those butterflies, and it is that fairytale feeling that is still there. It's the reassurance of love.

Quashaunda speaking: My husband and I can be total opposites at times. However, we know how to make it work. When it comes to love language, he is more verbal and visual. Because I love my husband and want to make sure I'm satisfying his wants and needs, I make a conscious effort to communicate to him in his (love) language. I like to say affirmative words to him, not just "I love you." I communicate how he makes me feel. I send him random text messages of my appreciation of not only what he does for our family, but also what he does for us. I know my messages make his day. Saying those sweet things really boosts his confidence and strokes his ego.

Because he often works out of town, we keep it spicy with those after dark late-night pictures or even videos! Listen, when it comes to understanding your partner's love language and wanting to please your spouse, throw being modest out the window. I give it my all!! When he is home, I'm selfish with him even to the point of our kids. I want him all to myself! Yes, we have family time, and we still even entertain friends, but I make sure I give him quality time, just the two of us going to some of our favorite spots, restaurants, sporting venues and music lounges. We love enjoying life together. Like our song "I'm M.A.R.R.I.E.D", says, "You can catch me at the house on the sofa watching movies. While I'm rubbing on his head, and he touching on my booty!"

Knowing your spouse's love language and exhibiting it will do wonders for your marriage. When you both practice the love language consistently and intentionally, it will ignite the passion back into your marriage. If this is a new space for the both of you, make it fun. Continue to date your spouse. It's such a treat when you can focus on each other without distractions.

For instance, I'm one who hates to get gas, and I don't like to drive. My husband will make sure that my tank is full before I get ready to go about my day or whenever we're going out on a date, running errands as a family, or going to church. I absolutely do not like to drive, and I don't even have to say a word. He automatically knows to get the keys and get in the driver's seat. That right there gives me so much peace and joy. I can just relax in the passenger's seat and sight see or take a nap. Again, it's the little things, and Will always has been an amazing father to our sons and to our now daughter, Kaydence, and also to his other daughters. He's been an absolutely amazing father. However, when we were apart and when we were in the process of getting back together, he made sure that he went above and beyond to do things in reference to the kids that I wouldn't even have to think about as a mother and as a self-employed woman in the beauty industry.

I am a licensed esthetician with a seasoned and growing clientele. The clients come regularly, which is what we want. However, depending on their lifestyles, they sometimes schedule late appointments. My weekends usually are for long days at work. During the week, certain nights I work evenings, so I can catch the nine-to-five crew and service their beauty needs when they get off work. I often get home late at night, or when I don't get home late, I'm still exhausted from being at work all day. Will makes sure the boys and Kaydence are fed. He makes sure homework is done. He makes sure the house is organized. It's not necessarily him organizing it. Let's just keep it real. The boys have chores, and Kaydence has chores too. It's all hands on deck! When I come home, I am much more at ease. I don't have to worry about what we're eating for the most part. Sometimes, I still cook when I get home. I still have to look over Kaydence's work sometimes because she wants me to check it. However, just knowing that I have a husband who wants to make sure he's doing those things, so I can relax and take a load off helps me trust that he has my best interests at heart. Those things really make a difference. Another one of my love languages is receiving flowers! It doesn't matter if it's a beautifully designed and delivered bouquet from a local florist or some of my favorites from the local grocery store. I absolutely love flowers, so he delivers them every week. That consistency and thoughtfulness is what is as beautiful as the flowers.

Wilber speaking: Fellas, let's be honest. Most of us don't require as much as our wives do in this area of love languages. I'm not saying that we don't have feelings or don't need to feel loved or be the little spoon at times. However, our love language is pretty simple, at least mine is. It's the little things Shaunda does like send those text messages throughout the day to let me know I'm on her mind. I love it when I get those pictures for my eyes only during the middle of my day when I'm ready to come home. That really does it for me. Because I am a man of affection, nothing beats a nice back rub and scalp rub/scratch. She gets it, and I love that about her. She's just as attentive to my wants as I am to her desires. The icing on the cake is when it's not forced but done with pleasure. Your spouse doesn't want you to feel like it's a chore to show them love. They don't want to feel like you'd rather be doing something else by the way you're acting. Don't feel bad if your love language list is longer or shorter than your spouse's list. Just be aware that they have one and act on it consistently and intentionally. Demonstrate enthusiasm with showing acts of their love language. That's what matters.

Here are the million-dollar questions. Do you know your spouse's love language? Do you practice it consistently and with pleasure? If the answers are "Yes" and "Yes," awesome! If not, you have some work to do, and we want to help. Make date nights a non-negotiable part of your passionate marriage. On your next date night, make it fun and productive. Start earlier that day or the day before and ask your spouse their love language. Leave all judgment and criticism behind. Write down your love language. On your next date night, share your answer with your spouse and talk about it. Discuss how loving you in your language makes you feel loved, secure, and desired. Your spouse's list may be two pages long. Don't get overwhelmed. It's okay. Create a daily or weekly schedule to implement their love language. Yes, we believe a schedule should be set. That keeps it intentional, and consistency is key. However, to keep it spicy and spontaneous, switch up what you do from their list and surprise them with each one. This shows that you are paying attention to their desires, and it shows that you want to fulfill them. You've gotten the foundation set, so now, this is the sweet spot. This is where the passion lies. Long after the wedding, you should date each other consistently. Seek to please each other and enjoy it. This intentional pursuit of your spouse will help you to stay emotionally and physically connected.

We made it!!! It feels so damn good. Now, our first marriage wasn't a disaster, but we had a lot of ish to work through. You name it, we went through it, literally. We experienced blended families, distrust, setting boundaries with co-parents and in-laws, financial hardships and more, but we made it! The space that we're in right now allows us to see and feel the difference in our love. It is so much more peaceful now. How? We did the hard work, which we talked about in these chapters.

Even though Will works mostly out of town, we are closer now than before our second time around. Our time spent now is mainly enjoying the fruits of our labor from building the marriage we desire to building and enjoying the house of our dreams. We still have the day-to-day activities of marriage; however, we take every opportunity to create beautiful memories. We plan our future and execute our plans. We strengthened our relationship with God as individuals. We pray with and for our spouse daily. We respect each other. When the disagreements come, we have learned how to keep calm, so we can find the solution. We own our mess!

If you're reading this book, then you're likely married and have made some sort of mess as well. This book will help you recognize it, and it will provide strategies to work through it. We are proof of how building a solid foundation looks. We've worked through a variety of different situations in which we had to regain trust in our marriage. Because we're humans, earning and regaining trust can be a revolving door, so we have to make sure our actions line up with trusting and not trying to control each other. Another key component is that we made the decision to go "All In." This time, we are more mature, and we have the wisdom of what it takes to have a healthy and passionate marriage. We're intentional about being present in every moment, the good ones and the difficult ones, knowing that we have what it takes to have the marriage we desire. We believe that this book will do the same for you and will be a guide to create the healthy and passionate marriage you desire.

Lord, Thank you for this life together. Thank you for the gift of our love and the blessing of our marriage. We praise you for the joy you've poured into our hearts through the bond of love we share. Thank you for our family and the happiness of our home. May we always treasure the experience of loving each other in our marriage. Help us to remain forever committed to our vows, to the promises we made to each other, and to you, Lord.

~Amen.

Epilogue

Now that you've read our book, *How Badly Do You Want It? A Married Couple's Guide To A Healthy & Passionate Marriage*, the marriage you desire is within your reach. You now have an action plan to implement these strategies. Improved communication between you and your spouse will lead to more peaceful, solution-filled conversations. Acts of your love language and intimacy will flow smoothly. The end-of-chapter prayers help to strengthen your foundation and bring substance to your marriage.

Your marriage is under attack. The constant arguing and lack of intimacy is drifting you and your spouse further apart. You've felt this way far too long. The quality of your life and peace of mind has started to go downhill. The cost of your peace of mind, your happiness, your household being split up, your children feeling confused and torn, and the divorce itself is a high price to pay. You have the power to change that. Do it now! You deserve peace, love, and happiness.

Once you implement these strategies and make the necessary changes, you will feel relief. You and your spouse will be able to rekindle the love you have for one another and achieve the healthy and passionate marriage you desire. In this book, you learned strategies to help you restore your marriage. Here's a brief breakdown. The following is a summary of the concepts that have been discussed in this book to heal and restore your marriage.

Chapter 1- Seek God First. This chapter teaches you the importance of keeping God in the forefront of your marriage.

Chapter 2 - Pray with and for Your Spouse. Here you learn to trust and believe in your prayers to God concerning your marriage.

Chapter 3 - R-E-S-P-E-C-T. This one can't be compromised at all.

Chapter 4 - Keep Calm. This chapter teaches you how to work calmly through your conflicts and get a solution.

Chapter 5 - Own It! This chapter teaches you how to take accountability for your mess and the environment it has created in your marriage.

Chapter 6 - A Solid Foundation. This chapter helps you understand how having trust in your marriage makes your spouse feel loved and secure.

Chapter 7 - Regain the Trust. This chapter gives you strategies that you'll be able to implement if your trust has been broken.

Chapter 8 - Distinguish Between Trust and Control. This chapter shows you that you'll be able to get a handle on issues of trust and control, so your marriage doesn't feel like abuse.

Chapter 9 - All In. This chapter shows you how when you and your spouse are on the same page, your marriage will benefit, and you will be drawn closer together.

Chapter 10 - Love Language. This chapter teaches you how to love your spouse in their language and how you can both celebrate and enjoy the fruit of your hard work.

The reality of a long-lasting marriage is that the Hollywood depiction of "being in love" and "butterflies in the stomach" is not 100% sustainable 100% of the time... Treasure it and be appreciative when the romance comes, but also know that the feeling of loyalty and commitment are even more satisfactory! Feelings are temporary, but being committed and honoring those vows give space and grace when our feelings don't always align; and it is always our path back to oneness. ❤

~ K. Trotter (female)

I would say learning to get over yourself. That's the easiest and hardest thing to do.

~ J. Harris (male)

About the Authors

Wilber and Quashaunda were band members at Southwest Dekalb High School. Over twenty-five years ago, they met in the band room where their love story began. Quashaunda has been a licensed esthetician in the state of Georgia for over fifteen years. She is the owner and licensed master esthetician of Complexions Skincare & Beauty, located in College Park, GA. She loves helping her client base of both men and women achieve their best complexion through treatment education and through her line of clinical skincare products and skincare essentials. When she is not working in her business, she loves spending time in her newfound passion of home décor. She and her husband, Wilber, have designed a luxury dinnerware and flatware set, which has been featured in one of Atlanta's top magazines, Modern Luxury Interiors, Volume IV in 2022. With art and creativity in her blood, Quashaunda loves creating five-star worthy meals for her family to enjoy with an exquisite presentation to match. Fitness is important to her, so when they designed their basement, her husband, Wilber, built a gym and added a sauna that she uses often. Her other hobbies include traveling, decorating, and dancing.

Wilber is in management with OSHA, and he is a real estate investor. His career causes him to travel a lot for work; however, they still keep the passion alive in their marriage. Quashaunda makes trips to go see him where he works, or he makes quick trips home between assignments. Since high school, Wilber has been into real estate. His mother introduced him to what a Beacon score was long before they ever flipped their first property together. Outside of working, Wilber is a real family man. He loves spending time with all his children, especially when they were younger. They would often go on outings where the kids could bond, enjoy each other, and eat together as a family. Wilber, dubbed by his family and close friends as the "Breakfast King," makes a breakfast/brunch to rival all breakfast and brunch spots. Their home is the place to be in the summertime when Wilber decides to get on the grill and cook his mouth-watering, fall off the bone ribs, aka "Wilba Wibs." Wilber's other hobbies include playing pool and golf, and he is very good at both sports. With cooking and a love for family in common, they're always entertaining at their beautiful home, and you definitely can feel the love. They also share a love for music and traveling the world together. They are enjoying their new role as grandparents, affectionately known as GiGi and G-Pop to their grandson. They live in Fairburn, GA with their children. To get more inspirational resources and to stay updated with future happenings, visit www.thekitchenstable.com.

∽

Love Happens Here.

Let's Get Back on Track!

Take aways:

_____

_____

_____

_____

_____

_____

_____

_____

_____

_____

_____

_____

_____

_____

From the bottom of our heart

"Thank You"

We are humbled and grateful that you purchased HOW BADLY DO YOU WANT IT? A Married Couple's Guide to a Healthy & Passionate Marriage.

Visit www.thekitchenstable.com to register your book and receive these exclusive bonuses:

- Access to join the Healthy & Passionate Marriage Program and receive $100 off the total investment.
- 25% off The Kitchens Table Luxury Dinnerware and Flatware Sets.
- One free 15 minute discovery coaching call with us.

Follow us on Instagram: @thekitchenstable2.0
Facebook: The Kitchens Table

Our song I'm M.A.R.R.I.E.D is available for download on all platforms ladyk.hearnow.com

Stay up to date and get more resources here:
www.thekitchenstable.com/sidenotes

www.ingramcontent.com/pod-product-compliance
Lightning Source LLC
Chambersburg PA
CBHW020331130626
46549CB00003B/1119